PRECARIOUS

PRECARIOUS

A Survivor of Clerical Abuse Remembers

PATRICK C. GOUJON, SJ

with a foreword by GERARD McGLONE, SJ
translated by JOSEPH MUNITIZ, SJ

Georgetown University Press | Washington, DC

The publisher is not responsible for third-party websites or their
content. URL links were active at time of publication.

Library of Congress Cataloging-in-Publication Data

Names: Goujon, Patrick, 1969- author. | McGlone, Gerard J., writer
    of foreword. | Munitiz, Joseph A., translator.
Title: Precarious : a survivor of clerical abuse remembers /
    Patrick C. Goujon, SJ ; foreword, Gerard McGlone, SJ ;
    translator, Joseph Munitiz, SJ.
Other titles: Prière de ne pas abuser. English
Description: Washington, DC : Georgetown University Press, 2023.
Identifiers: LCCN 2023016683 (print) | LCCN 2023016684 (ebook) |
    ISBN 9781647123819 (hardcover) | ISBN 9781647123826 (ebook)
Subjects: LCSH: Goujon, Patrick, 1969- | Jesuits—France—
    Biography. | Sexually abused children—France—Biography. |
    Child sexual abuse by clergy—France. | LCGFT: Autobiographies.
Classification: LCC BX4705.G617472 A3 2023 (print) | LCC BX4705.
    G617472 (ebook) | DDC 282.092—dc23/eng/20230530
LC record available at https://lccn.loc.gov/2023016683
LC ebook record available at https://lccn.loc.gov/2023016684

♾ This paper meets the requirements of ANSI/NISO Z39.48-1992
(Permanence of Paper).

24 23   9 8 7 6 5 4 3 2   First printing

Printed in the United States of America

Cover design by Brad Norr
Interior design by Matthew Williams

Dedicated to
the Pain Management Center,
Hôpital Saint-Joseph, Paris

Contents

Acknowledgments

In addition to those close to me, my thanks go also to all those who have encouraged me to publish this book: Marie-Charlotte Dalle, Patrick Autréaux, François Boëdec, SJ, and especially to Elsa Rosenberger of the Éditons du Seuil. Her kindly exigence allowed me to write what I wanted.

Many thanks to Joseph Munitiz (1931–2022), SJ, for his translation, to Gerard J. McGlone, SJ, and his invitation to publish it, and to Al Bertrand of Georgetown University Press for all his support and warm advice. The English version of this book has been slightly adapted by the author.

Foreword
Gerard McGlone, SJ

Throughout the globe at this time in our history, multiple and severe droughts are revealing many hidden and never before seen realities. Some are long forgotten monuments, rare dinosaur footprints, and whole Buddhist temples, to mention just a few. Sadly, the droughts have also revealed the dead bodies of crime victims, overturned cars that reveal long-sought missing persons, and World War II shipwrecks with live munitions and ordnance that need attention and care lest they explode. These discoveries are prompting many to begin to put words around the stories of these realities, these people, and these events that have long been forgotten, hidden, not known, or even denied.

The narrative you are about to read is one such reality.

I have read this book several times. Each time, I cry.

Reader, be forewarned. Most especially if you are a victim-survivor.

It is an honor and privilege to write this foreword. I first met Patrick Goujon, SJ, through a French Jesuit, Gael Giraud, here at Georgetown University. I met him virtually and still have not had a face-to-face encounter. His story fascinated me and his book, which was published in French, is now here in English. Here, you will meet an immensely talented man, writer, musician, theologian, and Jesuit priest. With all these talents and accomplishments, you will encounter a stunning ability first to know what happened, then to admit to this horror, and finally to find the words surrounding it. These are an entrance into the all too frequent series of realities for survivors of abuse. Survivors are amazingly resilient, and Patrick Goujon's story highlights the very depth and essence of resilience.

Goujon identifies for so many survivors the harsh, multifaceted, complex, and physically painful agony that is revealed when our personal droughts end and the seemingly endless storms, torrents, and rains of tears are shed. He reveals the amazing personal process and literal torture in putting words together, finding adequate words, and finally breaking the silence, the denial.

He was sexually abused by a priest.

Patrick Goujon's story is striking in so many ways. It's a rare glimpse of a recovered memory of being sexually abused. Scientific studies have confirmed the rarity of such an event.

However, its rareness cannot and will not allow the reader to deny it. It will surprise some and give hope to others. Rare medical cases occur every day. Their rareness need not and ought not bias the reader at all. If anything, the startling nature of how Patrick himself came to know his own abuse may help trauma survivors and those who have not experienced trauma better understand where the first impact of trauma most often occurs—the body.

Patrick invites us to see how, over decades, he struggled with severe and often debilitating back pain. One doctor finally said enough was enough with all the pain medications. That referral to a nontraditional pain management clinic set in motion a series of events: memories surfaced, doubts were confronted, cognitive inconsistencies and struggles overcome, and finally a truth that could not be denied any longer was embraced. The timing was, in a very real sense, painfully sacred.

The timing of recalling these events is also set in the backdrop of the work and stunning results of the Independent Commission for Church Sexual Abuse (CIASE) Report in France. Though controversial in the numbers that it estimated, the report is damning in detailing what has been described in numerous reports from around the globe about the atrocity of sexual abuse in the Catholic church. The members of the CIASE who were interviewed here at Georgetown detail a unique and troubling result. They observed consistent disregard of the victim-survivors but now with a callous and horrifying "lack of outrage" from bishops and other religious leaders. Consistent patterns of abuse, similarities in the types of abusers, institutional and organizational failures, the typical cover-ups, the geographical changes to protect perpetrators, and the failures of religious and diocesan leadership are so clearly detailed in this report. These realities are not isolated to one culture or country; they are and were seen all over the globe.

It is within this unique historical moment that we read Goujon's work. His story will outrage some readers in how the abovementioned realities show themselves in his pain, agony, and healing. Though rare in the research about recovered memories, this discovery shares many things in common to most of whom have struggled to believe, struggled to accept, struggled to find our voice and to find the words. Sadly, like so many cases, this one is still not settled in the juridical system. The church yet again has placed the perpetrator's needs, the institution's needs, above and before the needs of victim-survivors. There is the ongoing and unfinished outrage!

Precarious not only offers a chance to enter the process of finding the words to discuss being abused; it also is an entrance into the process of healing, enduring faith, and hope in the face of the horror of sexual abuse.

Precarious: from Latin *precarius*,
obtained through prayer.
Precari, to pray.

I recovered my voice when I was unaware I had lost it. As a child, I had been abused by a priest for several years. Then one day I found I could say this to myself, and I could speak. I had never imagined an experience like this could be so satisfying. I had to realize shame was simply a ghost and could not compare with the peace that comes when you are freed from these bonds. I had not known I had silenced myself.

I do not remember making the decision to stay silent: words were not there. For many years I had sought words, simply out of the instinct to survive. I admire those poets and musicians who know how to sing about silence. They have opened my ears. I had to delve deep into the heart of a pain that I thought had been gone. Fortunately, I have learned how to invent a life, to take it back, thanks to many encounters and experiences. That life has saved me. I chose to be a priest among fellow Jesuits. That happened almost twenty-five years ago.

For many years, I suspected something was hidden. But nothing could be seen, nothing could be said, until the day I decided to take care of my back. Or rather, others decided to take care of me and, gently, invited me to do the same. I could speak when I no longer had pain. I had to carry—I had been carrying—a deep secret, one embedded within my vertebrae, a cry that had been smothered before it could be uttered. By lightening up my suffering, others allowed my words to take shape. Words could escape at last from where they had been held captive. Through their repeated massages, their exercises, their liberating rubs, others used their hands as a lever. The pain at work in my spine finally rose to my lips. My words were pulled out from my painful muscles. They allowed me to become embodied and to choose freedom. My story could now find words.

I t was autumn 2016. I went to the emergency room with acute neck pain, and an examination confirmed I had two hernias. These hernias were in addition to three in the lumbar region. The doctor prescribed large quantities of anti-inflammatory drugs. The pharmacist was unwilling to give them to me until he had been assured by telephone that the dose was not excessive. The treatment hardly had any effect. The pain was spreading. Some weeks later I collapsed while in the street. My body would not go on any further.

I went to consult my primary care doctor. He was perplexed and wondered if I had a chronic illness. Then, almost as an aside, he said to me: "You've anesthetized yourself. Your body is protecting you from a collapse." His words struck me as if I had been hit in the gut. Without understanding fully, I knew my doctor was exactly right. I did not reply, but I was aware of my utter astonishment.

Over several years I had been canceling my classes, putting off arranged meetings. I had become afraid of long journeys, of changing beds while traveling. My nights grew shorter. Only swimming brought some relief to my suffering. At various moments of crisis, nothing seemed to help. I began to lose hope. People spoke of psychosomatic problems, but once they were mentioned nobody could help me further. My pains were classified as the imaginings of a hypochondriac. But if it was something psychological, I could not grasp what it might be. Apart from my physical suffering I was reasonably happy. I enjoyed my work. I was the director of degree programs in philosophy and theology at the Centre Sèvres, the Jesuit faculty in Paris. Also, I was busy with research into the history of the Jesuit order based on my seminar at the École des Hautes Études en Sciences Sociales. I felt I was at home in my religious life. My sole preoccupation was for the health of my mother, who had been hospitalized for long periods and whose health was getting worse.

The notion that I had anesthetized myself would not go away—however paradoxical it might seem—as I was still feeling pain. I was twisted into myself, wrapped around my spine. My muscles were strained. From childhood, my body made me suffer. How is it possible to curl up in this way when I'm over six feet tall? I always concealed most of what I was feeling. And yet intense lower back pain brought to the surface some obscure illness. I could see nothing in my past that would help me escape. During recent years, the frequency of the crises forced me to doubt myself and undermined my morale. It was as if the shock and pain from my sciatic nerve had enveloped me. A piercing toothache spread out for weeks into the rest of my body. And despite all this, I could not hear what my pain, my suffering, my body was trying to tell me. Instead, I did all I could with medication to silence what was being said. The pain had made me deaf. I was striking my head against a block and could hear the dull thuds, as if from a piece of wood.

I had an appointment with a rheumatologist at the hospital. He wanted to examine the state of my health in detail. He asked me how long I had felt ill. For nearly thirty years a series of spinal hernias and attacks of lower back pain had succeeded one another. My muscles seemed tied in knots. The rheumatologist turned away from the computer, where he was making notes. Before using the stethoscope, he listened to what I had to say. He allowed me to enter my past medical history. I was able to speak.

I told him about the back pain I had suffered from childhood. The pain went down as far as my pelvis. I had told my parents and the family doctor. It was not appendicitis. It was not important. And yet the pain worried me. The years went by. I was just someone who had a pain in his back. So I surrounded myself with a wall: no sports, and none of the games that children play. I was suffering. I was frightened of doing harm to my body. I was afraid.

When I was twenty years old, I was thought to be suffering from a rheumatoid illness linked with psoriasis, but the test results were all negative. When I was about thirty years old, some hernias were identified. However, the pain was out of proportion, and the symptoms did not fit the cause. I had run through the whole range of anti-inflammatory medications. One year a doctor advocated an anti-epileptic pill. Even opioids had been prescribed. They laid me low, and I had no wish to continue with them.

"Thirty years on anti-inflammatory drugs! They must stop! Do you mind if I take care of you? My plan is to direct you to our Pain Management Center. There we will try ear stimulation and hypnosis." I didn't need to be convinced of the benefits of osteopathy and acupuncture, both of which had done me much good for the last ten years. Unsatisfied with ordinary analgesic treatments, I had found various practitioners on my own. I left with new confidence and with some surprise that the doctor had recommended alternative medicine.

A few weeks later, even though I felt some hesitation, I went for my first appointment at the Pain Management Center. I had begun to think I was taking the place of a patient who really needed this sort of treatment. I was beginning to feel a little guilty. I wondered if I was not exaggerating my pains, and I began telling myself that, after all, my pain was not so bad. But I recognized this old story. The force of some recent crises brought home to me that all of this was misleading and unhelpful.

A doctor, smiling and very eager, greeted me. I told her I had been on the point of canceling the appointment. She assured me that sharp pain and chronic pain were two different things, and she added, smiling, that if I had been sent there, it was for a good reason. My scruples and self-judgments then vanished.

The first sessions of auriculotherapy (a form of acupuncture applied to points on the ear in order to treat other parts of the body) put an end to the massive inflammation. I was impressed. During the next several months, I met with many team members. I learned to use various techniques. I would anticipate a pain; I would treat it. I was caring for myself. That may sound very anodyne, but I was discovering the part I could play in my own recovery. I was not only a patient but an actor in my own story.

The hospital was only twenty minutes away from where I lived. I used to walk there several times a week. Far from interfering with my work, these breaks allowed me to breathe. In the waiting room, I was able to make more progress than ever in my reading as I prepared for my lectures.

I no longer felt pain. This was something quite new. And nevertheless, the specialists with whom I consulted were at a loss: the rate of inflammation could not be explained. For the time being, the doctors postponed more invasive examinations. I felt happy, with the feeling of breathing clean air after a heavy rainfall. There were no longer various pains to confuse me, to raise a wall or a screen between the world and myself. I thought I could get on with life like this.

W hen spring 2017 came, I set off for Rome in order to spend a few days working there. I made the most of the opportunity to visit an occasional museum or church, or simply to stroll. In one place the workshop of a violin-maker jutted into the street. It was as if I saw a shining glimpse of Baroque Rome. I felt enveloped in the shadows of Caravaggio and their crude realism.

One morning I decided to visit Saint Peter's Basilica to tour the excavations of the necropolis that contains the tomb of Saint Peter. It was dawn as I traversed the narrow streets of the city, and I stopped by chance to have an espresso in a café. Then I reached the broad avenue leading up to the Vatican. There was a kiosk where pilgrims gathered and were given copies of Psalm 121, the psalm of the exiles returning with joy as they glimpse the walls of the city.

As I read out the opening words, I heard, "Take care of yourself!" These words, first spoken by my doctor at the hospital, resonated as if, at that very moment, a voice were saying them to me. They were an invitation to be very gentle with myself.

I entered Saint Peter's to visit the excavations under the main altar of the Basilica. I felt welcomed by the silence as each of the visitors approached the tomb. A little later, a Capuchin friar heard my confession; at that time there were relatively few people in the Basilica. He comforted me for the distress and guilt I felt in putting up with my mother's infirmities.

That evening, I reflected in my room on the words I had heard in the morning. They seemed to lead me to a greater mystery than that of the tomb of Saint Peter. During those days I spent in Rome, I felt as if I was in a haven of peace, one suited to contemplation. I had no idea then what power would come from those simple words: "Take care of yourself!"

S ome months later, in October 2017, I was coming back from visiting my mother. After two days with her in the hospital, I was only too glad to cross Paris on foot, walking from the Gare de l'Est to my community house.

That hour-and-a-half walk gave me the chance to breathe deeply and to regain contact with ordinary life. I had made this walk often, and crisscrossing the streets made me feel better. I used to vary my route through the vieux quartiers, the old parts of the capital. I felt at rest with the calm and the freedom of movement. The rainy evenings had a certain gentle beauty. I was feeling much better and had practically no more back pain. In less than a year, the crises had disappeared, and I no longer needed any medication. My life had become much easier. My colleagues and companions in the community had begun to notice the change.

On that particular evening, I was aware that something still remained not quite right at the base of my spine. When I was under stress, some pain would return. I knew there would be a meeting I dreaded the next day. I was convinced my colleagues were refusing to face up to a problem raised by one of the teaching staff. When I thought nothing was being done to right this injustice, I fell into disproportionate fits of anger. My colleagues' denial made me angry.

I heard myself utter the word *denial*. Suddenly, there in the street, only a few steps from the Gare de l'Est, I felt a shock of electricity. *It was I who was in denial.* "Patrick, you well know what happened to you!" In less time than it would take to say it, that evil returned to my memory. As a result, my body and my mind, both brought to their true place, were no longer separate, but one.

I walked home as if I was walking on air, such was the joy I felt. Yes, real joy, however paradoxical that may seem. I had identified the evil: for too long I had held my body responsible for the suffering, but my body was not poisoning my life. I had been feeding it with drugs to muzzle it. I had treated it as something that needed to be put right with all sorts of orthopedics just to keep it quiet. The etymology says it all: *orthos* (right) and *paidos* (of the child). That type of medicine was not what was needed. Instead, the child had to be led toward speech; the child had to emerge from one "who does not speak" (*infans*) to one given permission to cry out for help.

"Do you mind if I take care of you?" the rheumatologist had asked me. I had gone in through the door half opened for me. Something came to an end that day. Death had left me. But what was to follow was to be an ordeal.

D*eny*: those two syllables had been confused in my mind with *forget*. But denial is not forgetting: it preserves. The suffering does not disappear; it has nowhere to go. The suffering disguises itself; it buries itself. The denial is at work; it makes the entire body grind. Denial compresses. It breaks up the pain into small pieces. Denial scatters itself through body and soul. It takes up residence where a weakness appears: back pains, childish fears, a loss of freedom.

Denial intercepts an emotion that would be too violent. Some power of the psyche is at work and raises a screen. But the victim is not really saved. There is the trap: denial protects for the moment but inserts something else that will cause suffering for twenty, thirty, forty years. The victim is unable to identify suffering's origin: it has been camouflaged so that the child may grow.

Denial shatters the memory and pulverizes it. The wound relocates itself into a sequence that cannot be rewound; there are images that cannot fit into any story. In the end, traumatic experiences fade away, as there is no desire to bring them back into one's memory. During my adolescence, I had buried these experiences without even being aware of what I was doing. We all prefer to move on from what does us harm.

Nevertheless, aggression is there. The slightest thing can revive it. I had become volatile. Various times of the day were particularly difficult: shadow puppets could alarm me. A nightmare would arise for no reason. There were times when aggression came to the surface, but it was wearing a mask. My soul was thrown into confusion. I hated walking along a corridor in the dark. One evening, it was only by forcing myself with all my strength that I could look behind me. There was no one following me.

Denial makes the monster into an unrecognizable revenant. It throws a veil over what would otherwise be too horrible. That horror could destroy. Denial protects because it shifts the horror aside. Such support is short-lived, for denial brings harm. No matter how helpful denial may be, we should not forget that denial is rooted in the violence of a crime that defaces tenderness and confuses love with abuse.

When I reached my room after my walk from the Gare de l'Est and closed the door, I asked myself if I had been making things up. I was terrified at the thought that this sudden remembrance might not have been true. Was I or was I not a victim of a horrible crime? For the next six months, I did not know what to do or what to think. Was it true?

Yes. I knew it was. My recognition had been clear, the liberation I had felt was too intense and long-lasting for me not to be sure. But the force of the denial struck me as incredible. Reason forced me to hesitate. How could such a void be hollowed out in my consciousness? And how could I not have noticed such an emptiness? If I had reached such a degree of blindness, how many more unknowns were lying in wait for me to discover? I was afraid I might glimpse at the edge of the forest some wild beast normally hidden in the darkness. I felt shackled by these and other questions. How, and why, had I hidden such assaults in my memory? Who had done it? I could not remember having made the decision to forget. I trembled at the thought of this underground activity that had escaped me.

For many months the shame of having been defiled never left me. A priest, for almost three years, used to masturbate against me. The sense of culpability was not slow in arriving. I had said nothing. Was it because I had something to conceal? Had it given me pleasure? What had I, as a child, experienced? I was haunted by this thought. Within me a wall had been erected: You will not have access to that scene. You will not go back to what has destroyed you.

All of this was very confusing as I reflected on it. These thoughts tangled up my nights. They were a background noise to my days. I took some time to note them down. My daily life had become strange. I was carrying out my duties as director of studies. I began work on a new book, studying the history of spiritual conversation. Work brought order to my life. Being busy saved me from a collapse. I rose early in the morning so that I could have moments of calm in which to write. My days at the Centre Sèvres passed as if all was in order. The lively friendship of my colleagues was a support for me, even if I was not always patient with those who came to me with their own problems.

The decline in my mother's health increased my anxiety. Living alone in a care home for a long time, not without serious moments of crisis, she longed for my daily short phone call. I was happy to hear her but often felt at a loss on hearing her recount, quite dispassionately, the phases of her ordeals. I had to struggle not to feel sucked down by her suffering. Along with my brother and his family, I gave her support. I was particularly careful to ensure time for myself to be alone, something necessary for each of us but so difficult to find, even in the life of a Jesuit. When evening came, after my shared meal with the community and the prayers we sang together in the chapel, I would find myself caught once more in the middle of a battlefield. Quite often, to delay the struggle, but also to give myself something of a respite, I would watch a movie, either alone or with some of my companions. Silence, meditation, and serious reading helped me. I was exhausted.

The truth, which had dawned on me in a moment of illumination, effectively broke up what I thought was my identity. The truth had exploded the fabled account of my childhood with its mixture of genuine happy moments. I now found myself facing a mirror smashed in the center, in which reflections made no sense. Those cutting edges made blood run. For many long months, I felt I would not be able to reassemble the pieces. Each day brought a new understanding of some feature of my personality. But I could form no idea of the overall picture this puzzle was showing me. I had no model to guide me, and this scattering of pieces was anything but a game. My history was presenting me naked to my own eyes. How ugly I looked. I found it difficult to accept what this revelation had opened up. I had to learn how to accept, gently, what nobody else would ever desire.

I said nothing about all this to anyone. I was working out secretly how I might confirm my intuition without revealing it. Had I been the only victim? Was the aggressor known for similar acts, in other places and at other times? I was twisting myself into knots in this pseudo-investigation in which I could ask no one to help me. I was at the same time detective, witness, and counsel for the prosecution. Nothing was coming to light. How could I establish the facts? Why speak of it at all? And to whom? Should I prosecute? How could I avoid slander? To whom could I mention the name of the priest without arousing suspicions? Would I be causing scandal? What would they say, the Catholics I knew? Public opinion in 2017 was still very far from being ready to hear this story, and some Catholics have never understood the need to help victims and to prosecute the guilty. Some would misinterpret what I was doing, and I did not want to accept the consequences of these misunderstandings. My thoughts went back and forth without end. So confused were they that I felt incapable of doing anything, of coming to a decision. At least this long-drawn-out process prevented any sudden action at a time when I felt so fragile.

My first task was to take on board the incredible violence committed so that I might dare to spell it out plainly. I had to struggle against my own incredulity. The only point of certainty was the paradoxical joy I felt on the evening when I remembered.

A thousand thoughts continued to buzz in my head. They exhausted me. Six months I had already lived in this torment without revealing it to anyone. I had taken the risk of attempting to share something with one or another of my fellow Jesuits, but without success. The questions continued to envelop me in their web. Then one Sunday morning—it was, I remember, Easter Sunday—I was in the sacristy of the chapel in my mother's hospital. I happened to ask one of the priests, "Do you know Fr.——?" "Oh, that nightmare? I'll just tell you that all my life I've had to deal with pedophile priests. Back in the 1950s, the bishop sent one of them to lodge with me before he was transferred to a house in the center of France . . ."

I had not been raving. That priest was known for his abusive attacks. So I was right. I could stand on my two feet, alive.

That afternoon I went to visit my mother once more in the hospital, and I took with me some madeleine cakes that I had baked for her.

A few weeks later, in November 2017, I decided to write to the bishop of Verdun about this pedophile priest in his diocese. I did this with some hesitation. One of the Jesuits I trusted had recommended not to stir things up. But I felt very strongly the opposite: I had to speak out. From that Easter Sunday, I had been regularly seeing a psychologist who helped me. After a long moment of silence, I finally came to the decision, feeling exhausted but not defeated.

One evening during my prayers I resolved to write to the bishop about the facts and the identity of the priest who had abused me. I slept better than usual. I got up early to write the letter in the calm of the morning. In my room I had only to walk a few steps to my desk. I sat down, but my heart was not at ease. Why should I write? What good would it do to raise all that up again? I especially felt that I was not free.

Suddenly, I felt a hand pushing me from behind and forcing me to sit down at my desk. I could not be a traitor to myself. "I believe, therefore I will speak." Psalm 116 came back to me just when I was on the point of running away. I opened my computer. What followed was a struggle against chaos.

After a few words of introduction, I felt I was buried in a volcano and had lost control of language. Nothing seemed real. I had to force myself up, pushing my head above the lava. Never before had I made such a physical effort. I could hear myself bawling, like someone drowning in the roar of a flood. Subject—verb—object. I clung to that. I looked for the most ordinary words to express, to write. I had the feeling I was carving words onto a block of hard marble.

I explained to the bishop what had happened to me. A few words were enough: more were impossible. I felt I had to make clear that for a long time I could remember nothing, even though in my adolescence I had understood what had happened to me. Very briefly, I described the sense of liberation I had felt when at last I acknowledged the repeated abuse.

I stumbled over the name of the priest: I could not bear to give him his title, *monsieur l'abbé*, "reverend father." I was not able to utter his proper name. The infected vowels and consonants seemed to escape me. Why were they so elusive? Although I checked after writing them down, I had to verify the spelling when I needed to give his identity. To my child's ear the letters of his name either slipped or felt sticky. That's how it is. That's enough. I had no desire to hold the name close. I didn't want it to be stuck to me anymore.

I was not completely satisfied with my letter, nor was I sure that there would be a reply. Still, I put a stamp on the letter and sent another copy to the bishop in charge of the agency responsible for child protection in France. The latter called me the next day. As for the bishop of Verdun, he received me a month later. I had been heard. He had notified the public prosecutor about my case. "Go right on!" he encouraged me. "I will support you."

I wrote at once to the public prosecutor. It was an easier letter to write. I had found out how to do this thanks to the Ministry of Justice website, which explains how to lodge a complaint. I lodged one against the priest, claiming that he was guilty of abusing a minor. I couldn't afford to make any mistakes in this process. I forced myself to find out the details about a legal prosecution. A little later, a magistrate confirmed I had done what was required.

All of this exhausted me. Yet from this time on I felt happy and sure. At this time, I was also accompanying my family to visit my mother in her final months.

There was a transformation in my prayer life. I recovered the joy of a period spent in the community chapel as night fell.

Kneeling at the foot of a medieval crucifix I loved, I waited at a distance for Christ to pass in silence, as He thought best. I settled quietly. I paid attention to my breathing, as singing has taught me. A seated posture helps and settles. The prayer moves along at floor level. It comes from deep within. The body has to discover how the soul may come to find what it is looking for.

A verse from the book of Isaiah came to my mind: "And the wolf will dwell with the lamb, and the leopard will lie down with the young goat, and the calf and the young lion and the fattened steer will be together; and a little boy will lead them" (Isaiah 11:6). I could see that child, at peace, happy and serene; he was reconciling the savage beasts with their prey. Sweetness and savagery were combined. I decided to follow him so that he could finish his work.

During the following weeks, in December, I would go to meet that little boy again each evening in my prayer. Suddenly, I was that child, and at the same time I felt carried by him. I took the child whom I was upon my knees so that he could rest and guide me. The little boy of Isaiah, the child whom I was, and the adult who I am met that Christmas night. The Child was carrying me. I felt strengthened in the joy of telling the truth, with a minimum of words and silence.

S ome weeks later, in January 2018, my phone rang. It was a police officer. The public prosecutor had passed my case to him. Although I was expecting the call, I could hardly believe my ears. I was afraid that I would be considered guilty. Without my knowing it, my fears had made me illogical.

The police officer's questions were precise and respectful.

Then he asked me, "Could you come to lodge your complaint?"

"I am going to stay with my mother who only has weeks to live."

"In that case I shall go and ask the prosecutor if we can see you at the police station near your house. It would be pointless to burden you with this while you are visiting your mother."

As I put down the phone, sitting in my armchair, I felt overwhelmed. It was as if I had been sucked down into the abyss and then risen to the surface just in time. A cry had suddenly brought me up out of the chasm I had fallen into.

At that very moment, aged forty-eight, I had gone back to my childhood. At long last, I had heard the cry that had, for so long, been trapped in my bones. Simply giving it voice brought me back all at once to life. A shout, the voice sounding out, with a kind of rust in that cry. I collapsed.

But immediately, without the slightest noise, the child I had been came to console me. He thanked me for having dared to follow this path. A mighty wind had carried me. It allowed me to be born a second time.

I had decided to act. I would prosecute. Through this process, I would put things back in their rightful place. The word *crime*, which is part of the vocabulary of justice, allows you to refer to abuse in a way that avoids overwhelming trauma. The law shifts the point of view. Until then, I had not acknowledged the seriousness of the abuse. Thanks to the abstract vocabulary of the penal code, the plaintiff discovers at last that he is not alone in rejecting what was imposed on him. The law forbids it. In France, "sexual abuse is defined as any violent attack committed with violence, constraint, menace, or surprise." This prohibition authorizes the plaintiff. He has the right to denounce. The law justified my malaise. On the other hand, I can acknowledge the truth of my pain and not be trapped in the role of a whiner: "Alas, no one will ever be able to console me!" As La Fontaine mockingly said in *Fables* XII.26, "There's always a touch of show mingled in our tears."

I did not want to complain and feel sorry for myself. I was living. I had found consolation despite the harshness of a situation which had left me helpless. Surely the joy that had pulled me clear from denial could not find expression in a prosecution. And yet I had to disentangle myself from the overtones of that word. The decision to prosecute had prevented my going back to the child enclosed in silence. I had dared to utter a *precarious* word. My memory of what had happened was partial, faulty. I cannot say if there had been witnesses or other victims. I am not the only one who knows the truth about what happened to me. But this is true: I have been abused, and I know who did it. The wounds are still with me. For a long time, I have suffered. True, the memory of what happened is defective. To live, you have to be able to forget. The victim must pay the price of haziness in those memories. The victim's testimony can be weak sometimes. The power to speak, which has cost so much to regain, is full of doubts. Yet you must not allow uncertainty to undermine the determination to speak out. You must have the courage to denounce the crime and to identify the person responsible, even if you also recognize that you do not know everything about what happened. I made the decision to speak out about it.

To make a formal complaint at the police station was an ordeal for me. I had to recapture precisely what had happened. Had I seen his penis or not? Did he hold mine? I had to give the names of witnesses, the other priests who may have been aware of what was happening, those priests then living in the parish. One of them had helped awaken my vocation. Tears came to my eyes. These were questions I had not encountered before. There was no longer uncontrollable weeping, but there was emotion in this act of recalling, a glimpse of my childhood. I appreciated the tact of the young woman, the police officer (called in French "the guardian of the peace," *gardien de la paix*, such a beautiful name). I thanked her. To help find the truth, I had to speak out, to tell things as they had been, at least according to my memory, without shame nor fear. By making the complaint in a police station, I was detached from the emotional context and could concentrate on the narrative. I was able once more to move out of myself. A cold, difficult, process, but it allows some distance and is beneficial. Tears may come, but the time for sobs has passed. To hold on to your pain at this stage is no longer to deny it, but to shift it so that you may speak.

I was no longer alone on this path. I had placed my hope in justice, that it might help me. However, making this complaint had triggered a new tension: I waited a year and a half, until March 2019, for the prosecutor's decision.

Once I had denounced the abuse, I thought I had put it behind me. I thought I could put the memory in its proper place. And yet it was impossible for me to live without it. I realized one day I was on the alert constantly, or nearly so.

I never sat down with my back to an open door. I was always afraid someone would break in. I was paralyzed. As a child, I had been frightened I would no longer be able to walk. At that time, I had symptoms that soon vanished. Once when I had the flu, at the time I was being abused, I no longer had the strength to get up. My legs were giving way. The family doctor had mentioned Guillain-Barré syndrome (the name struck me to such an extent that I have never forgotten it). He swiftly ruled out that diagnosis after a few tests, but it continued to haunt me during my childhood. I wonder now if my body was not using tricks to draw attention to itself.

The child does not close the door against someone who comes to cuddle him. That is how he is abused. The definition of that word, given in French by the famous dictionary *Le Robert*, says it all: "To *abuse* someone: to possess a person who is unable to refuse it." And what follows makes one shudder: "To use something until it disappears."

I am on the alert: I can see what is coming. I feel the manipulator on the prowl. He wants to reach you without your permission. He enters. He helps himself. He takes because he only wants his own pleasure. As for me: I withdraw into myself; I hide within myself. May it not start again. Being on the alert is exhausting, but I hear the approaching footstep: "He's there!" The relaxation comes, but slowly, gradually advancing.

I had recovered the power of speech, but I felt serious tension. I was starting on a new life; nevertheless, it did not look at all like what I had imagined. My body kept track of what my memory had lost.

What happened to me as a child had not been painful. Hadn't it been like my relatives cuddling me? Except that the abuser pushed me away as quickly as he had grabbed me.

My body became twisted and folded. My diaphragm felt crushed, the solar plexus compressed. To protect the center, the peripheries had become pressed together. I found myself in a state of shock. The anxiety never went away.

My skin felt raw, flaky. I became overweight. The muscles seemed to contract until they tore apart. Inflammation. Thrombosis. The bones crammed together. The spinal disks contracted. Hernias. Difficulty falling asleep. I had to hide under the blankets with plugs in my ears. Avoidance of all noise. Footsteps: who is after me? A light appears: who is coming near? There was a feeling of stress, insomnia. There was a deep anger, but I could not identify why. It had no face.

And now, hypertension, stomach problems, always without any recognizable illness. The doctors repeat: "Hyper-emotional symptoms." They may harm your health in the decades to come. And yet I take time to look after myself. I must practice stretching. One hundred times a day, the job of relaxing must be undertaken. Morning, noon, and night. My body continues being tense, as if it is always closing inwards to protect me.

I don't think I suffered in this way twenty or forty years ago. The wear and tear showed itself only during these last few years. Can I quote the dictionary *Le Robert* once more? It is a real treasure: it makes clear how common what is happening to me. *After-effects*: "the consequences, the complications that can be felt sooner or later, and may last for a long time, of an illness or accident." Will those who do not understand why victims reveal themselves so long after the "supposed" cases of abuse listen to this dispassionate lexical voice? Think of the archaeological remains that rise from the soil or, at Verdun, the live artillery shells of World War I that threaten to explode in one's face if handled without precaution. By speaking out, I had withdrawn from that minefield.

As a child, I had been aware of various symptoms. They gave no signal; no one had linked them to one another. My body was expressing itself, but I had not spoken. The insomnia I suffered in my adolescence or the trembling that shook me awake had not suggested to the doctor some hidden trauma. Such a diagnosis did not exist at that time. I had learned to live as I was. From my imageless anguish I had peopled my dreamless nights. Then one day I overcame my fears, timidly at first. But surer of myself, I came to see how good that was. People were wrong about the sort of person I was. I had no choice but to rely on myself even when that was impossible for me. I discovered that there were crossing points available because freedom was calling out to me to take them, and I was encouraged I had taken the risk.

I tell myself I have been lucky. One female relative whom I loved is dead, because she had been the victim of her father's abuse.

I devoted myself to following the criminal case. Justice would free me from evil. I placed my hope in the judicial process, a hope it could not fulfill.

I was waiting to find truth that was not at my disposal. I wanted to understand what had happened and read about the facts in an investigative report. I was tired of being alone with my memories, my fears, my impressions, and my deductions. The law speaks without emotion so that what is right can be heard without giving way to scandal, horror, or overwhelming anger. At that point, the victim does not need the emotion of others. Her desire is simply to recognize the facts that can be named: aggression, offense, crime.

Time passed slowly. I had cast off the illusion that justice would rid me of my fear. Perhaps I had imagined that at long last I would revisit the scene. When interrogated, would the abuser express some regret that I would be told about? Or the diocese, would it somehow apologize and confess how seriously it had been at fault? Would there be reparations (though I had no idea what form that might take)?

Nothing was clear to me. I was aware of what had happened to me. I had also a vague idea that about ten years after the abuse, the priest in question had been relegated to the diocese offices. As an adolescent, I happened to meet my abuser, and I had the impression, on the few occasions when we looked at one another, that he was undergoing treatment. He seemed dazed. He walked hesitantly like someone using sedatives. Had action had been taken? Where had he been sent, as he was no longer seen in Verdun? Was it all just gossip that I had heard and that was coming back to me now? Justice would set right all that was troubling me. Justice would reveal the facts and sort out what had really happened to me, what I had guessed, and what I was reconstructing to fill the blanks in my just-recovered memory.

What was known about the culprit? (The bishop had in fact told me: "Priests of his generation all knew about it." So he was a repeat offender; I had not spoken about him to anyone. That was what I understood, what I deduced from what was said to me.) It was not *proof* of what had happened that I needed— it was long ago, witnesses had disappeared or their memory had become faulty. I needed a narrative of the facts.

I wanted to be informed. I needed an objective report in the midst of my turbulent thoughts. At times I worried, and at other moments I felt calm because there would be an objective report, at least as much as there could be nearly forty years later. My state of mind might seem strange, but I believed an account of the facts would calm the growing fever of not knowing exactly what had happened to me.

In March 2019, a year and a half after my complaint, I received a letter from the prosecutor. The case was closed: the time for initiating legal proceedings had run out. However, he added a note: "It is possible for facts to be acknowledged by the perpetrator, but the victim's rights cannot be enforced owing to the statute of limitations." This clarification was a great help to me: the facts were acknowledged.

To make a formal complaint had been useless. It was only at this point I felt indignant with those who had done nothing earlier. It had not been enough to reassign that priest. He should have been arrested by the police after his first offense. The day I received the prosecutor's decision, in March 2019, I called the bishop of Verdun to inform him about it. I gave no sign of my anger or of sadness. I felt paralyzed but forced myself to be polite. He told me that he would be writing to the Congregation for the Doctrine of the Faith, which was responsible in the Vatican for dealing with these cases. Only bishops can initiate such a procedure.

Less than an hour later, I wrote an email to a priest I knew in the abuser's diocese. I was fairly sure he knew a thing or two. When I was about eighteen years old, I had asked him for news about my abuser, probably hoping that he would give some hint of any rumors or suspicions. I feel I would have been able at that point to speak out. He only answered vaguely, so I had not risked going any further. But thirty years later, I was no longer afraid to ask clearly. He replied right away.

His opening words were enough: "While I was in Verdun it was said that N—— had been appointed to the diocese offices to 'keep him away from children.'"

So I had seen things correctly. I had been uncertain, ever since the memory had returned, whether I had the capacity to feel and understand what happened to me as a child and afterward. I was afraid of losing my balance, my sanity, and no longer having a hold on reality. It was absolutely necessary for me to be sure of what I was feeling. Yes, I had really seen that the priest in question had been moved to another role without punishment.

Why was it, the day before receiving this letter, that a very definite memory had come to me in a dream? It was the first time that the person who had abused me actually appeared in my dreams. It did not happen in a nightmare, but rather in a recollection, a return to the original scene.

At the time I was being abused, my father and I would sometimes on a Sunday afternoon visit the Cathedral presbytery. My father had spent some time in the hospital with one of the priests, and they had become good friends.

On the night of my dream I remembered that N—— was staying with that priest. But what stuck in my memory was that when we arrived, N—— fled from me. And the deep unease I felt as a child came back to me. Why was this man, who had clung to me in the morning, now avoiding me in the evening? That discomfort was still with me as I awoke. I recognized that unmistakable feeling, the steely coldness that still froze me. In the morning, I had been caught in a trap, but in the evening, I could see the falsehood for what it was. His avoidance, which made me wonder then, now shows clearly what had happened. The child had glimpsed the abuse that, at the moment it was happening, escaped him.

With the reception of that email, things changed. I was now completely sure I had been a victim and that my lawsuit was credible.

My rage: I was on the point of not saying anything about it. I am ashamed of it because it torments me and turns me into anything but the peace-loving person I want to be. It is present, like molten lava beneath the surface. When it erupts, I suffer.

I fly into a rage in certain situations. And so I have been able to decode my denial. I can't stand it when somebody in a position of authority commits an injustice. It's even more impossible for me to tolerate denial of some abuse. My rage explodes when the voice of the victim is not heard, yet again. I feel that I am suffocating, in the literal sense of the term. My breathing is blocked. There is a hand over my mouth that stops me from speaking. My rage bears down on me because I glimpse the shadow of the oppressor at work.

The most recent example of this? It's almost comical. One of my colleagues, a professor, told off a staff member because there had been a mistake in reserving a lecture room. The person in question had nothing to do with it. The rebuke made me crazy. In these situations, I have a one-track mind: reason doesn't come into it. Here's someone small being torn to pieces by someone big who cannot be stopped. The strongest will always be right, as La Fontaine wrote in his fable "The Wolf and the Lamb."

These situations occur again and again. Or rather, to my eyes they repeat themselves. My fits of anger have often made things worse. Because of them, I become unjust myself. I have probably exaggerated the harm being done, magnifying it. I carry on as if, I was the one being ill-treated. My attempts to cool my fits of rage with a dose of kindness are difficult. This distresses me.

However, the struggle with my rage would not worry me so much if it were not linked at the same time with my inability to find the words. Furious though I may be at some injustice, I often find myself silenced. The way the church has shown itself to be deaf to cases of pedophilia enrages me. Its silence often makes those who have been victims incapable of speech, because of their shame and suffering. Admittedly, the church has made some genuine efforts, but the arrogance and the lack of empathy shown by some in authority appall me. They pay no attention to those who have been afflicted. This is what I find impossible to accept. It is not enough to have followed the canonical procedures. There is a need to taste the bitterness of such crimes and to bear some of the shame that weighs so heavily on the victims. I wish I could control my rage without losing the determination to speak out.

W hat dismays me was that I did not know how to talk about this for so many years. Here I was, first a literature professor, then a theology lecturer, a preacher, the author of several books. I had been studying how the *Spiritual Exercises* of Saint Ignatius of Loyola still encourage the freedom to speak. And yet I had kept silent. How could I have passed by my own life to such an extent? Had I deceived myself? Had I not been an impostor? That was what I was tempted to think. I felt dizzy when I thought of my own blindness. That long training—as a Jesuit, as a professor of literature, as a theologian—which should have taught me how to listen, how to speak, how to give spiritual direction, had it all been useless?

When I was a child, I often liked to spend an evening leafing through the dictionary. I explored its hidden treasures. But was that reading not simply a vain attempt to come across words I had been incapable of speaking? My love of literature was invaded, like a worm in an apple, by my longing to hear and speak out. At first, the realization of what had happened to me had been a liberation. But with time, it became a corrosive acid.

Yet how many horizons had opened up for me through my reading and led partly to my choices in life? Was it not because I had browsed my way through the Bible that I had elected to share its liberating grace and power? My impression now was that I was distracted by the speech of others instead of trying to set free my own power of speech. I had gone adrift. Suddenly, I saw that literature suppressed my own ability to speak. Had I not been looking for my own words in what had been written, when first of all I should have been opening my mouth? Suddenly, the passion that had led me to great literature and the rigor I devoted to its study were all in question. The books in my library had become nothing but ashes. Not only did I suffer knowing how much I was a victim, but I also felt all that supported me melt away. I was on the point of collapse.

By chance, at that time some professional circumstances brought me back to my university career. A colleague pointed out a link between my present work devoted to the nature of spiritual conversation and my first thesis, written some thirty years earlier. This thesis was on the *Fables* of La Fontaine. My colleague noticed that both dealt with the opportunity of individuals to speak. The remark astonished me.

I knew that my fondness for the *Fables* dated from my childhood. I had discovered La Fontaine when I was about seven years old, thanks to a gramophone record I liked to play repeatedly.

Un lièvre en son gîte songeait

(Car que faire en un gîte à moins que l'on ne songe?)

(A hare in his lair did dream

For what else does one do in a lair but dream?) (Fable II.14)

I had entered then into the musical universe of the poem. Just a few syllables were enough to put me under the poem's spell. Surrounded by poetry I had built my own den. I was protected by my family environment and lived happily with the poet's cheerfulness. The monster lurking at my back was relegated to the rank of the ogres in the stories. I would take the risk of emerging, glad to meet other people. Like the hare in the fable, I had overcome any fear:

Il n'est, je le vois bien, si poltron sur la terre
Qui ne puisse trouver un plus poltron que soi.
(No coward upon this earth, I see
but can find another more cowardly than he.)

But now I had recognized the monster and could no longer take refuge in any poem. While my colleague was talking to me about my earlier work, he was unaware that the *Fables*, which had engendered my love of literature, overlapped with the silence that had so burdened me. I nearly staggered when I heard him say that the *Fables* were an illustration of the precariousness of the spoken word. "It's useless to utter prayers," he had added. As I remembered the melancholy evoked by La

Fontaine, I felt driven into a corner. No! It was that very precariousness that had created in me an ear and a voice. It had not been a total loss. The fable held out for me the promise of speech.

"**A**nd nevertheless, today you're a priest! How is that possible?" the police inspector had asked me in an aside. My reply came out immediately: "I believe in God." Now that I look back on it, I am surprised I replied like that. The upheavals of the last few years have allowed me to go back to that answer. Why had I chosen to become a priest? Ought I to remain one today? Although I have been happy in my vocation, I felt compelled to ask the question. I wanted to know the truth about my decisions. But hard work was needed.

I do not know what first awoke my vocation when I was a child. I have been told that very early on I said I wanted to be a priest. I do remember one thing for certain: there was something there. This longing came to me. I received it as a suggestion, as an invitation to be considered. I had to get accustomed to it. I tamed it. Somewhat later, when you begin to recognize what you want in life, I had the impression I could help my friends at school by listening to them. I was astonished to find that there was a clear echo between what they told me of their lives—for some of them this was really painful—and what I found in the pages of the Gospel, which I was reading at the time. It was not the miracles or the multiplication of loaves, but that they were solutions even if situations seem to be hopeless. Jesus of Nazareth set free those crushed by a sense of guilt or burdened by the accusations of others without wanting to put a load on them. Faced by those in authority at that time, He was free to denounce religious hypocrisy and spoke out in defense of those who were being forced to keep silent. Then He Himself was condemned to death unjustly. How could I not be attracted to this message?

It was not a god I saw in Jesus, but a sage who could be described as a saint. I was not very inclined to believe in an all-powerful god. The books that formed part of the school syllabus encouraged my distrust: the ironic belief of Candide in "the best of all worlds" and the wisdom of the Stoics provided the best answers to my adolescent questions. I was overwhelmed by Camus. His "saint without God" in *The Plague* seemed to be the summit where Christianity was leading me. I felt in tune with the credo of Dr. Rieux: "I have no liking, as far as I can see, for heroism or sanctity. What interests me is to be human." I could have adopted that confession as my own.

However, I was transfixed by the compassion of the God Moses had discovered in the burning bush. "I have certainly seen the oppression of My people who are in Egypt, and have heard their outcry because of their taskmasters, for I am aware of their sufferings" (Exodus 3:7). This phrase does not solve any problems, but it shook me. It turned me back toward God and made me discover Him in other ways than I had imagined. God allowed Himself to be shaken and did not dwell on some Mount Olympus overhanging our earth. Despite all the mythical trappings that can be attached to the story of His son, His end was not something you would wish. Could not a father who was God have come to His help? And yet there was no sudden miracle: the son was to die on a cross. And we all have to die. The fact that Christianity recognizes death is what saves it for me. From then on, I could learn with its help how to cope with my humanity, holding fast to the hope that death will not end everything. Fortunately, the first books of theology that I was lent—there are some good ones—encouraged me to continue. It was a moment when the church was no longer preoccupied with the frontiers between believers and nonbelievers. Rather, it was the life of all that held its attention.

After much hesitation, I could see that the priesthood was the path I should take. However, there were many other projects that attracted me. I could see myself becoming a competent teacher in a school or college. I fell in love. I had difficulty imagining myself in obedience to a religious superior or to a bishop. They were years when I swayed. My final school exams were approaching; as I studied, I was brought face-to-face with my fundamental longing. Yes, I did want to teach, and I could be a researcher and a professor, but I could not go back on my former attachment to God. He was drawing me with a sort of magnetic force I had felt since childhood.

However, there was something faint, hardly a glimmer, the red tabernacle lamp. I had understood as a child that the lamp was simply a piece of staging, a bulb, not even a real flame. And yet it was a sign. It appeared to me to be linked, truly for once, to the world's beginning, not to an idea without a face, but to the Name, the one my parents had gently taught me to utter at night before going to sleep. Such a small thing. Years later a verse from the Bible strengthened me with its bracing terseness: "And a dimly burning wick He will not extinguish" (Isaiah 42:3). Those words had kept me going in the faith.

Did I ask myself, without my knowing it, "But where was your God when you were being abused?" I cannot answer that question. I never believed that God keeps us safe from violence, and I found confirmation of this in the fate of His son. But He does listen, and that is how He saves. Job was beseeching his friends, always ready to instruct without hearing him, "Listen carefully to my speech, and let this be your way of consolation" (Job 21:2). Any consolation that only tries to show the cause of a suffering is illusory. The inaction of God is a trial for us. I believe that is the hidden face of His care.

It was never my conviction that the abuse inflicted on me should not have happened *in church*. Already as an adolescent I understood that the church is not exempt from any of the evils perpetrated by humankind. The church's crimes simply raise the only question worth asking: how can I, one among others, face up to the violence that I can see at work among men and women, in myself, and even among those who profess an ethical code of loving one's neighbor? As long as the Catholic church—to speak of it alone—believes it has been freed from evil, the church is on the wrong track. While believing in the church, we are called to recognize that evil is at work in it, as in any human group and in each of us. It is only too obvious that the conscience of each of us is divided. That division may become clear with the deliberate choice of some wrong action, but it can be glimpsed when one of our decisions hides in the dark, and we think a failure to choose what is right will pass unnoticed. Our only hope is that evil will not set a seal on the final condemnation of us all. That, I think, is what God is saying with the faith of Christians. Far from imprisoning us all under a sentence of guilt, He implores us to set aside what prevents us from living. Our responsibility is restored. "Sin is lurking at the door; and its desire is for you, but won't you master it?" (Genesis 4:7). Cain would have heard this voice before the murder of his younger brother, Abel. The conscience of each of us can hear the same question.

The sexual abuse of children found at the heart of the church is a scandal; it is, moreover, a crime. It strikes down the smallest, and some never recover. Everything must be done to prevent it happening. In that way we will learn once more that as Christians we share the fate of a humanity torn by violence. Like everyone else, we all share the same hope for peace.

It is not difficult for me to grasp why some would not want to have anything to do with this faith. The scandal of abuse seems to disprove what the church promises. But I have not been able to renounce hope, though I have seen its light flicker at times. My sole prayer is that I may not forget how closely linked are darkness and light.

Healing takes a lifetime. I am learning not to rush anything that might blossom someday. But the waiting is painful. I feel I am completely powerless to pardon. I do not say "incapable"; nor do I say "unwilling." The word I use is "powerless."

Abusive conduct kills. It destroys little by little. I do not have in myself the power to re-create what has been ruined. I am able to live. For that, there is no price. Can there be a greater joy? I live, but with wounds. They have made me understand that death has been at work within me. Death does this to everyone. But my death has a criminal face. I can live with scars, but I do not have the power to re-create what has been destroyed.

If I forgive, it won't be enough. The original promise has to be found once more: each of us will be able to live and love. Pardon is linked to creation. I do not have this power at my disposal. I ask God for it, a God who I hope will forgive my abuser. I don't know how that will come about. I hope for it.

But voilà, occasionally I pass on the street gray men, in scruffy trousers, puffy-faced, with small steel-rimmed spectacles and a haggard look. For many years such an appearance made me feel hate. Obviously, this emotion was not directed against these unknown individuals. It was a hate that did not have a target; it spread within me, deep in my gut, and eventually it found an outlet in some inappropriate remark. Only recently have I made the connection with the likeness to the man who abused me. Now I can disarm that hate because I know its origin, and I have no desire to let it proceed. For too long it has exhausted me with its wanderings. In order to live, one must set aside the wish to destroy.

I dare not imagine how that man, in his fifties when he committed the abuse and now nearly ninety, spent the rest of his life with those crimes on his conscience. I would be pleased if he were allowed to discover his crime. Might I ever hear his apologies?

A child would say: "I don't want that man to go to hell. May God keep him from that."

"If you forgive the sins of any, their sins have been forgiven them; if you retain the sins of any, they have been retained" (John 20:23).

I saw I was waiting for him to ask for forgiveness so that I might grant it. I was not able to deny my wound, but I had no need to hang on to it. I was set free from the part of me still resisting. At that point I was no longer attached to my assailant, as I had a strong wish that he might thirst for forgiveness.

My psychologist has helped me to resist the temptation of thinking my whole life has flowed from abuse and owes nothing to my own choices. With her I have gone back patiently over my life. I was on the point of giving way to despair: it could so easily have carried me off into the darkness.

I felt I had the right to reconsider my previous decisions, to face making them afresh with the freedom I had rediscovered. I am convinced I have received the strength to confirm my decisions, firm in the desire to continue living my life as it is, not with a bitter sense of resignation, but with the peace that accepts things as they are.

At long last I felt proud of the child, the adolescent, and the young adult I had been. I felt proud of the choices that allowed me to move ahead. This pride is not an attempt to evaluate success, to pass judgment on myself. I can feel joy and pleasure in what has been life-giving.

I have resisted fear by daring to listen to my wishes to go out and meet others. This desire would not seem extraordinary, except that it meant crossing the barricade erected by sexual abuse. I felt shame; I had a damaged image of myself that had to be hidden. To survive, I relied on what others saw in me. This fact has never ceased to astonish me. I would never have believed in myself without my school and university teachers, friends, priests, and literary and musical mentors.

I was twelve years old when for first time I heard a soprano singing a few feet away from me. The sound of her voice resounded and was transformed into pure bliss and happiness. From then on, I wanted to sing. I would practice at home and also in the school choir. A little later, when I was twenty years old, I met a distinguished professor. He suggested I become his pupil when I least expected this. He taught me the requirements of style and the happiness it brought. Later I entered a musical academy and profited from some excellent lessons given by a great teacher there. My voice could joyfully hand me over to others. I had no idea what those musical mentors heard that deserved so much encouragement.

I am not alone. To trust in what I desire, to learn how to express it, to risk it with those I live with: that is what has saved me. One's longing is, so to speak, like God. It never allows itself to be fully grasped. Like Him also, it gives life. In the *Spiritual Exercises* of Saint Ignatius one can avoid the trap set by wanting something straightaway. Thanks to the *Exercises*, I have learned how to speak the language of my longing in order to address the Absolute, the One whom nothing can bind. And then, as when the Word brings cosmic order to primeval chaos, handing over my longing to God allows me to be born into the world as it really is.

The child in me has been courageous. I decided it was not good to seal up my longing. "You have chosen what saves you," my psychologist said to me one day. "Well, I didn't 'save' myself by running away," I replied. I could have fled. I did not. Denial made an appointment with me for later, when I would be able to put a stop to it. I had not saved myself because another is saving me.

He, also, has taken care of me.

Will you allow me, for a moment, to say something more about Him? He is a kindly Shadow, who guides especially when night is falling or some worry takes hold of body and soul. He gives off a light that one must learn to recognize. Our human flesh allows us to see Him only in a faint glimmer.

Caravaggio shows a soldier covering Jesus with a tunic when Pilate presents him, *Ecce homo*. The clothing veils the violated body. It protects. It spares the viewers any sight of the wounds. Caravaggio is painting the body of God in the flesh of violent humankind. Traditionally that cloak is thought of as made of royal purple, a unique item, a single piece of clothing, seamless. Jesus is unique.

God provides clothing for all of us. As Adam and Eve were ashamed of having sinned, God sewed them clothing. His love is a cloak that shelters me from the shame of having been a victim of abuse. I have wanted to help others so that they can choose the clothing God offers them. For God has seen that we cannot hold out in such a state. He has opened a workshop and invited creative couturiers, models, clever hands to work there. Styles are varied, updated to suit each person. The divine hand in this can hardly be seen, so close does He keep to our human bodies and human desires.

However, all too often, little is needed for shame to return. I distance myself from that shame, so useless, empty, and false: it has nothing to do with me. I am not the guilty one. I am aware how profound is my deafness, the difficulty I have in believing I have been saved. Not a refusal, but slowness. For constantly the murmur of fear comes back.

To be silent and to accept you have no defense. What a sweet haven! The place where you can rest. I did not need a protective cover. I had no fear of falling to pieces. Without a mantle, yet not dismantled.

I was feeling better. It was spring 2019. The reply to my questions had come not from the prosecutor. Instead, I received an email from a priest I knew in Verdun. Now I could trust myself. I had been right in my feelings. I was learning how to decode in a different way something of what I had felt. My fears had sometimes been like a magnifying lens. The pain in my body had stopped. Yet I continued to be restless in character, and there was a risk of inflammation due to my damaged tissues.

One day I was surprised in the course of a conversation with a friend. He was aware of what had happened to me. I don't remember exactly how the conversation reached this point.

"But you know, Patrick, that I love you."

"Well, really, I'm very fond of you as well."

This friend then took up my remark, which was unusual—he would normally let a conversation flow.

"No, I didn't say I was fond of you, but that I love you."

I did not interpret this as a confession of love, a sort of "I am in love with you." Rather, it spoke of a relationship that dared to speak its name. And his words shook me. I felt that whisper of fear that always prevented me from believing that the love I felt for him, and for others—men and women—could be reciprocal. I was afraid this sort of love was to gain control over a person. But a terror sprang up then, only to disappear. It had prevented my loving anyone without my realizing it.

I perceived for the first time how love can have a sort of density. I was aware how particular was that link that attaches one person to another and is not to be confused with either esteem or affection. So great had been my fear of loving that I had preferred not to believe I was loved. I knew I had been loved, but I found it impossible to believe. I was realizing how suspicious I had been, even in my most intimate life. With that insight, I could believe the person who said he loved me.

With that it dawned on me just how perverse any abuse is. It distorted my thinking that love was not to be desired or sought after, that I had to protect myself against love. As if any declaration of love foretold a treachery. If love is truly to receive the beloved in one's flesh and to want to embrace the beloved, abuse made me afraid that relationships could be nothing but possession and would inevitably end in crime.

With full clarity it is written: "We have come to know and have believed the love which God has for us" (1 John 4:16). Faith touches what is most vulnerable in each of us. Faith means believing love is where one can find solace and a home, even while it constantly opens us to be vulnerable. The scandal of pedophile priests is a violent attack on this central aspect of the Christian faith. Their abuse attacks the point where faith is most promising and uncertain, the point where trust is indispensable.

I have chosen to be celibate, and without doubt this is because I want to attach myself to God. I can accept this. I would not want to pretend afterward that there was nothing in it of fear. I can accept that too. The realization came to me one day when my osteopath was touching me. He has been taking care of me for nearly twenty years. The contact of his hands, quick and chaste, made me feel I would not have allowed anyone else to touch me. In his case, I was happy to let him.

There is nothing to be gained from pretending that a man who chooses to be celibate is free of all struggle or illusion. The talk of the ancient monks in the Egyptian desert about various carnal battles shows that the celibate do not think less about sex. Those monks did not want to minimize either its violence or its attraction. Saint Anthony in his arid hermitage used to call the forces that pass through us "demons." While invisible, these urges are proof of the chaos from which life is drawn. However imperative they may be, they teach us nevertheless how we are to behave. They listen to one another, they interact, but they cannot be denied. They provide the rhythm to both life and death, and from them existence is born. Night and day, their sway echoes constantly. The celibate person may well increase the resonance. And the celibate person who lacks these movements of flesh and blood would be eerie. My body is attracted by the bodies of others, for there is always more to the body than can be seen. The appeal may be powerful. It is also possible for me to reduce the other to a mere object. With all my wounds and my desires, my choice has been for this life of solitude, within a community, and I have chosen it once more in the joy that celibacy gives to love and to be loved. I accept being alone, though the weight of that loneliness may be heavy. I have learned to acknowledge celibacy has also been a refuge. Were celibacy to turn in on itself, it would no longer represent what I am hoping for: namely, a symbol of my preference for the One who cannot be grasped. With a faint glimmer, which has not gone out, He manifests Himself. I believe.

All too easily, people have forgotten that religion affects both soul and body. If I were to search for God only with my soul, I would feel I simply want to discover an image, an idea. I need some physical signs—the silence of a church nave, the sweet stillness of a crypt, a radiant sun, a loving heart. The outstretched hands help the soul to root itself in the quest. The God who comes to us is made of flesh and breath. The search for Him does not exile a religious person from his body and from meeting with others. Being celibate simply makes one more patient for God.

ne morning in March 2019, the bishop of Verdun called me. Rome had given him permission to open a canonical inquiry. I was delighted my experience would not remain private. My experience involves a diocese, other persons, priests who were in place at the time, those who were aware of other cases, witnesses, and quite certainly other victims. For me this new development did not mean halting the civil prosecution according to some sort of ecclesiastical privilege. Canon law also has a statute of limitations, but at least a preliminary investigation was beginning. It seemed to me the diocese would be given the chance to shed light on the cases of abuse that had been committed within it. While the guilt always remains with the aggressor alone, the responsibility is that of the church and its leaders.

Nevertheless, I began to feel at once a certain fear. This was not only because I would have to give testimony once more, but also because of my concerns about the very process itself.

The church became both judge and prosecutor. The investigation would be carried out by the diocese where the events had taken place and under the supervision of priests who were at the time holding office. Eventually, the bishop alone would have the duty of drawing up the case file for the Vatican. Why not entrust the investigation to others, independent from the case? Also, the inquiry would be focused once again on the aggressor, without any questions about the church's inaction in the face of his known crimes. The church's internal law should evolve more in this regard. In addition, both the clergy and the faithful should weigh our responsibility to protect victims and denounce aggressors.

At least with this new stage the prosecution I had set in motion had not been in vain, nor had it been only for my own benefit. It seemed to me other priests would both speak out and speak to one another. But what a mess. The two priests who came to question me told me what they had known about that priest forty years ago. They shared with me, in all honesty, their scandalized embarrassment. However, this sort of confession is of no help to victims.

To understand the ecclesiastical process, I had to immerse myself in canon law. I learned that a preliminary inquiry is not a prosecution and that there would be no final judgment or sentence. It's an administrative process, not a judicial one. The bishop sent his report to Rome in January 2020, and it was his duty to punish the priest. "That priest will not be able to celebrate the sacraments," he told me when he called again a few months later. Some may find this punishment ridiculous, while for others it will seem excessive. However, such a sanction makes sense in a world where being a priest makes you untouchable.

In June 2020, there was a new development: a criminal investigation was set up to examine clerical abuse for the entire Verdun area, and other victims of this priest were found. My hope then was that the diocese would reply to this new investigation. It is not enough to allow the victims to speak out and to set up counseling centers. The wound must be bandaged by an acknowledgment of the depth of ecclesiastical responsibility.

In July 2021, a civil judge interviewed me. I read the reports of the civil investigation. Even today, in January 2023, the investigation is still ongoing, and I cannot reveal anything about it. I can say only that after reading the extent of the priest's other crimes and of ecclesial complicity, my immune system imploded: lymphatic system, asthma, and paralysis were the results. Anxiety froze me for several months.

In October 2021, the Independent Commission for Church Sexual Abuse (CIASE) commissioned by the French Catholic church released its report: its findings included countless sexual assaults, and a systemic responsibility of the Catholic church (see recommendation 24). The president of the French bishops' conference has welcomed the conclusions. I was shocked by the figures—three hundred thousand victims (as many as the French dead in the battle of Verdun during World War I)—but I was encouraged by the determination of the commission and the way the report resonated in French society. There has been no bashing of the church—which might have been predicted in our secularized country—but instead there is a common understanding of the need to deeply transform the church. Yet resistance to change within the church has been expressed. The commission's figures were challenged, as were its recommendations for safer protection, its suggestions for training priests about sexual issues, and the need to review canonical procedures. Some priests or laypeople refuse to accept that an outside commission should invite changes in the church. The Bishops' Conference of France, however, have officially accepted the report's conclusions. The results may be long in coming, but significant decisions have been made. Commissions for reparation have been created by the bishops and the religious conferences, as well as a national ecclesial tribunal.

1977 ... 2017 ... 2023, and my case is still pending. But, as far as I am concerned, something has definitely changed. I know I can speak. A child can bear the word.

It's tempting through this rough process of healing to neglect the love and the joy given to me before my memory came back. It's clear enough as I reread these pages. Denial protected me by wrapping in oblivion what I undoubtedly could not have borne earlier. My memories came back at the right moment. Evil came knocking at my door at a time when I could resist.

When I was more than forty-five years old, there came a sudden landslide that carried me off. I needed to scan my entire life to find what had survived. Certainly, I found corpses of my anger. However, I have been fully living all these years. I can't consider that all has been an illusion, a covered-up wound, or a lie.

I cannot deny my joy. My friends would not recognize me if they did not read about what supports me—my singing, my studies, my delight in teaching, my life as a Jesuit, and the love of those whom I meet and to whom I hope to be of some service.

Nor am I able to erase that paradoxical joy that arose when I spoke the two syllables *deny*. The sound of my vertebrae, so well-known and so agonizing, took on a new form of speech. Again, joy seized me when the name of the man who had abused me was said by someone other than myself. I was not crazy. I was saved. A prosecution was brought forward. My words allowed others to speak up, those who no longer believed it possible to live among other people.

I did not realize that joy can cost so much. The church's resistance to denouncing evil threatens my joy. I hope, however, not to let this joy be taken away from me. I hope not to be overcome by this burden any longer. It will be a struggle. But a child will keep watch.

So I put together a prayer:

May our ears hear the pleas

And our eyes see the paralyzed bodies.

Let us decipher the murmurs;

May we take the risk to speak, however precarious.

The children will rise to lead us.

Patrick C. Goujon, SJ, is professor of spirituality and theology at Centre Sèvres–Jesuit Faculties in Paris. He is also the chief editor of *Recherches de Science Religieuse* and a fellow at Campion Hall, University of Oxford. He writes on the history of Jesuit spirituality and has published *Counsels of the Holy Spirit: A Reading of Saint Ignatius's Letters* (Messenger, 2021).

Joseph A. Munitiz (1931–2022), SJ, was editor and translator of Byzantine texts, a founder of Corpus Christianorum in Translation, and also editor and translator of *Ignatius of Loyola: Personal Writings* (Penguin Classics, 2005).